JENELLE AUBADE

Modern Lampwork Recipes – Fire and Glass by Jenelle Aubade

Volume 1 – Jubilee

First published by Star Dust Writes 2023

Copyright © 2023 by Jenelle Aubade

All rights reserved. No part of this publication may be reproduced, stored or transmitted in any form or by any means, electronic, mechanical, photocopying, recording, scanning, or otherwise without written permission from the publisher. It is illegal to copy this book, post it to a website, or distribute it by any other means without permission.

Jenelle Aubade asserts the moral right to be identified as the author of this work.

Jenelle Aubade has no responsibility for the persistence or accuracy of URLs for external or third-party Internet Websites referred to in this publication and does not guarantee that any content on such Websites is, or will remain, accurate or appropriate.

Designations used by companies to distinguish their products are often claimed as trademarks. All brand names and product names used in this book and on its cover are trade names, service marks, trademarks and registered trademarks of their respective owners. The publishers and the book are not associated with any product or vendor mentioned in this book. None of the companies referenced within the book have endorsed the book.

First edition

This book was professionally typeset on Reedsy.
Find out more at reedsy.com

"In the right light, at the right time, everything is extraordinary."

- Aaron Rose

Contents

Preface	ii
Acknowledgement	xxi
About Jubilee	1
Jubilee Round Duo	4
Jubilee Barrel	13
Jubilee Organics	18
Resources	24
BONUS : Additional Design Examples	29
Afterward	34

Preface

Overview of Glass Bead Making (Lampworking)

Welcome to the enchanting world of glass bead making, a realm where creativity meets the elemental dance of fire and glass. Often referred to as lampworking, this art form is both ancient and ever-evolving, offering a unique medium for artistic expression.

What is Lampworking?

Lampworking is a fascinating glassworking technique that involves melting rods of colored glass using a torch, to shape and mold them into beads, figurines, and other decorative objects. This process is performed at a lampworker's bench, equipped with a flame that is fueled by a combination of gas and oxygen.

The heart of lampworking lies in its ability to transform glass into intricate and detailed designs. By manipulating the molten glass with tools and hand movements, artisans create beads and other objects with diverse patterns, textures, and colors. Each piece is a testament to the skill and artistic vision of its creator, making lampworking a deeply personal and expressive art form.

Lampworking vs. Other Glassworking Techniques

While lampworking is a part of the broader glassworking world, it holds a distinct place due to its technique and outcomes. Unlike glassblowing, which is often associated with creating larger items like vases or bowls, lampworking focuses on smaller, more detailed work. This precision art requires a steady hand and a keen eye for detail.

Another key difference lies in the equipment used. Lampworking utilizes a bench-mounted torch for heating the glass, which offers more control for detailed work compared to the larger furnaces used in glassblowing. This makes lampworking particularly suited for creating intricate beads and miniature sculptures.

Moreover, lampworking allows for a more intimate and immediate interaction with the glass. Artists work directly with the material in its molten state, shaping it in real-time. This direct engagement with the medium provides a unique sense of connection between the artist and their work, which is less pronounced in other glassworking techniques.

In summary, lampworking stands out in the glass art world for its ability to create detailed, intricate pieces with a personal touch. It's an art form that combines skill, creativity, and a deep understanding of the material, resulting in beautiful, handcrafted pieces that are as unique as their makers.

Historical Context of Lampworking

As we delve deeper into the realm of lampworking, it's essential to appreciate the rich tapestry of its history. This journey through time not only informs us about the origins and evolution of this craft but also connects us to the generations of artisans who have shaped it into the art form we know and love today.

Origins of Lampworking: Ancient Beginnings

The roots of lampworking stretch back to ancient civilizations, a testament to the enduring allure of glass as a medium for artistic expression. Historical evidence suggests that the earliest forms of lampworking may have originated in the regions of the Middle East and the Mediterranean, particularly in areas known for their glassmaking expertise, like Syria and Egypt.

In these ancient times, craftsmen used simple tools and a flame source, likely an oil lamp with a controlled flame, to manipulate glass. These early lampworkers set the foundation for the intricate beadwork that would become a hallmark of the craft, creating small yet significant glass objects that were treasured as personal adornments and trade items.

Evolution Through the Centuries

Over the centuries, lampworking evolved alongside advancements in technology and artistic trends. During the Middle Ages, the craft continued to flourish, particularly in regions like Venice, which became renowned for its glass artistry. The development of new tools and techniques allowed for greater precision and creativity, leading to more elaborate and refined designs.

The trade secrets of Venetian glassmakers were closely guarded, but knowledge eventually spread across Europe, inspiring a diverse range of local styles and innovations. Lampworking became a prominent craft in countries such as Germany, France, and the Netherlands, each adding their unique cultural touch to the art.

The Renaissance: A Pivotal Era for Glass Art

The Renaissance period marked a significant turning point in the history of lampworking. This era, known for its explosion of artistic and scientific discovery, saw glass art reaching new heights of sophistication and beauty. In Italy, the Renaissance ignited a passion for artistic excellence in glassmaking, with Venice remaining at the forefront of innovation.

During this period, lampworking was not just about crafting utilitarian items; it became a means of artistic expression. Glass artists began to experiment with color, transparency, and form, creating pieces that were as much about art as they were about function. The intricate beads and delicate glass sculptures from this era are still revered for their craftsmanship and aesthetic appeal.

The Renaissance also saw the spread of lampworking knowledge beyond Italy. Artists and craftsmen traveled across Europe, sharing techniques and inspiring a new generation of glass artisans. This cross-pollination of ideas contributed to the vibrant and diverse landscape of lampworking that we see today.

By understanding the historical context of lampworking, we gain a deeper appreciation for the art form and its place in the tapestry of human creativity. This rich heritage serves as both inspiration and foundation for contemporary lampworking artists, who continue to push the boundaries of what can be achieved with fire and glass.

Lampworking Today

In the vibrant and ever-evolving world of lampworking, the traditions and techniques of the past blend seamlessly with modern innovations and creative explorations. Today's lampworking stands as a dynamic art form, continually reinvented by new technologies, materials, and the boundless imagination of its practitioners.

Modern Techniques and Innovations

Modern lampworking has transcended its historical confines, embracing a wide array of techniques that push the boundaries of glass art. Contemporary artists employ various methods such as 'flameworking', using high-temperature torches to achieve more precise and intricate designs. This evolution has opened doors to an unprecedented level of detail and complexity in bead designs and other small-scale glass creations.

Innovations such as the use of borosilicate glass, known for its durability and resistance to thermal shock, have expanded the creative possibilities. Artists now experiment with a spectrum of colors and textures that were once unimaginable, crafting pieces that are as robust as they are beautiful.

Transition from Traditional to Contemporary Practices

The journey from traditional lampworking to its current form is marked by both continuity and change. While the essence of shaping glass in a flame remains unchanged, the methods and tools have undergone significant transformation. Today's artists stand on the shoulders of the past, drawing inspiration from historical techniques while infusing their work with contemporary flair and innovation.

This transition is evident in the way modern lampworkers approach their craft. There is a greater emphasis on personal expression and artistic freedom, moving away from the production of uniform beads to the creation of unique, one-of-a-kind pieces. This shift reflects a broader trend in the art world, where the focus is increasingly on individual creativity and storytelling.

The Role of Technology and New Materials

Technology has played a pivotal role in the evolution of modern lampworking. Advanced torches and kilns allow for greater control over the glass, enabling artists to achieve more precise results. Tools such as digital temperature controllers and sophisticated ventilation systems have made the process safer and more efficient.

The introduction of new materials has also revolutionized the craft. Apart from the expanded palette of glass colors, the use of metals and other elements in the glass mixture has led to the creation of stunning effects and finishes. Additives like mica, silver, and gold leaf are used to create shimmering surfaces and intricate patterns within the glass.

Moreover, the integration of glass with other materials, such as metal for jewelry settings or incorporation in mixed media art, showcases the versatility of lampworking in a contemporary context.

Lampworking today stands as a testament to human creativity's adaptability and endless potential. By embracing both the rich heritage of the craft and the possibilities opened up by modern advancements, today's lampworkers continue to enchant and inspire, pushing the boundaries of what can be achieved with fire and glass.

Lampworking as an Art Form

Lampworking stands out as a medium where artistic expression knows no bounds. Each piece, from a simple bead to an elaborate sculpture, is a canvas for the artist's imagination. The process of melting and molding glass into intricate shapes and patterns is akin to painting with light and color. Artists bring their personal style and creative vision to life, making each creation unique and reflective of their artistic journey.

The flexibility of lampworking allows for an extensive range of styles – from the whimsical and abstract to the meticulously realistic. Artists can experiment with color combinations, textures, and forms to create pieces that resonate with personal narratives or artistic themes. This expressive potential makes lampworking a deeply personal and emotionally resonant form of art.

Significance of Lampworking in the Broader Context of Glass Art

In the broader context of glass art, lampworking occupies a special niche. It represents a blend of technical skill and artistic vision, showcasing the versatility of glass as a medium. Lampworking artists often push the boundaries of traditional glass art, introducing innovative techniques and ideas that influence the field as a whole.

The art of lampworking also plays a crucial role in preserving and evolving traditional glassworking techniques. By keeping these age-old methods alive and relevant in a contemporary setting, lampworking artists ensure that this rich heritage continues to inspire and inform future generations of glass artists.

Materials and Tools

Modern lampworking is characterized by a diverse array of materials, each offering unique properties and possibilities:

1. Glass Rods and Tubes: The primary material in lampworking, available in an extensive range of colors and compositions. Borosilicate

glass, known for its durability and heat resistance, and soft glass with a wider palette of colors, are commonly used.

2. Colorants and Frits: Used to add hues and textures to glass. These come in the form of powdered or crushed glass and can be mixed or layered to create varying effects.

3. Metallic Inclusions: Materials like silver, gold, and copper are used to create metallic effects within the glass. These can be in the form of leaf, foil, or wire.

4. Millefiori: These are cross-sections of glass rods with intricate patterns, used to add detailed designs to beads and other creations.

5. Enamels and Paints: Applied to the surface of the glass, these materials are used for adding intricate details and additional color layers.

The Evolution of Tools and Equipment

The tools and equipment in lampworking have evolved significantly, enhancing the capabilities of artists and the safety of the craft:

1. Torches: The heart of the lampworker's bench. Traditional oil lamps have been replaced by modern torches that offer precise control over flame size and temperature. These torches use a combination of gases like propane or natural gas and oxygen.

2. Kilns: Essential for annealing, a process that strengthens and stabilizes the glass. Modern digital kilns allow for precise temperature control and programming, critical for complex projects.

3. Hand Tools: These include tweezers, mandrels, marvers, and tongs,

which have evolved from basic designs to ergonomic and specialized tools tailored for specific tasks in lampworking.

4. Safety Equipment: Modern lampworking emphasizes safety, with the use of ventilation systems to remove fumes and protective eyewear designed to shield artists from harmful infrared and ultraviolet light.

5. Workstations: Contemporary workstations are designed for efficiency, comfort, and safety, accommodating multiple tools and materials, and ensuring that everything the artist needs is within reach.

The materials and tools in modern lampworking are a testament to the craft's evolution, marrying tradition with technological advances. This fusion not only broadens the creative horizons for artists but also ensures the sustainability and safety of this beloved art form.

Safety Considerations

While the art of lampworking is filled with creative joy and the satisfaction of crafting beautiful glass pieces, it is imperative to approach this craft with a strong commitment to safety.

1. Proper Ventilation:
   - Importance: Working with hot glass generates fumes and gases that can be harmful if inhaled. Proper ventilation is crucial to remove these from your workspace.
   - Implementation: Use a professional-grade ventilation system that directs fumes away from your breathing zone and out of your working area.

2. Eye Protection:
   - Importance: The intense light produced by the torch can be harmful to your eyes, potentially leading to "glassblower's cataract."

Special glasses are necessary to protect against infrared and ultraviolet radiation.

- Type of Glasses: Ensure you're using didymium or polycarbonate safety glasses specifically designed for lampworking.

3. Handling Hot Materials:

- Heat Safety: Always be mindful that the glass and tools can become extremely hot. Use appropriate tools to handle hot materials and never touch anything that's been near the flame without proper protection.
- Cooling Down: Have a designated safe area for cooling down hot glass items, away from any flammable materials.

4. Proper Clothing and Workspace Setup:

- Clothing: Wear natural fiber clothing (like cotton) to minimize the risk of burns. Avoid loose sleeves and dangling jewelry.
- Workspace: Keep your workspace clutter-free. Ensure all flammable materials are stored safely away from the torch area.

5. Gas Cylinder and Torch Safety:

- Storage and Handling: Store gas cylinders upright and secure them properly. Regularly check hoses and connections for leaks.
- Torch Maintenance: Regularly inspect your torch for any signs of damage or malfunction. Follow manufacturer guidelines for usage and maintenance.

6. First-Aid and Emergency Preparedness:

- First-Aid Kit: Keep a well-stocked first-aid kit readily accessible in your workspace.
- Emergency Plan: Have a clear plan for emergencies, including how to shut off your gas and electrical supply and a route for quick evacuation if necessary.

7. Educating Yourself:

- Continuous Learning: Stay informed about best safety practices. Attend workshops, read up on safety materials, and engage with the lampworking community to learn about new safety advancements.

Adhering to these safety considerations is not just about preventing accidents; it's about respecting the craft and ensuring that the art of lampworking can be enjoyed for years to come, free from preventable harm. Safety is the foundation upon which all successful lampworking is built.

Section 7: The Importance of Technique and Skill

In the realm of lampworking, the journey from a beginner to an intermediate, and beyond, is not just a matter of time or practice, but a continuous pursuit of mastery over technique and skill.

Mastering Fundamental Techniques

1. Foundation of Success:
    - Role of Basics: Fundamental techniques form the bedrock of lampworking. Mastery of these basics, such as maintaining a steady flame, understanding glass properties, and controlling glass flow, is essential for creating quality work.
    - Building Complexity: Advanced techniques are often extensions or variations of basic skills. A solid grasp of the fundamentals allows for more intricate and detailed work.

2. Precision and Consistency:
    - Developing Steady Hands: Techniques like bead shaping, pattern making, and color application require a precise and steady hand, which is developed through consistent practice.
    - Consistency in Work: Consistent practice leads to consistent results,

a key marker of skill in lampworking.

Journey from Beginner to Intermediate

1. Overcoming Challenges:
   - Learning Curve: Transitioning from a beginner to an intermediate level involves overcoming challenges, experimenting with different techniques, and sometimes dealing with frustration and setbacks.
   - Problem-Solving: Each challenge presents an opportunity to develop problem-solving skills, crucial in advancing your lampworking abilities.

2. Exploration and Experimentation:
   - Trying New Techniques: As you progress, experimenting with new techniques and styles is vital for growth. It expands your creative horizons and enhances your skill set.
   - Personal Style Development: This phase is also about discovering and refining your unique style, which becomes more pronounced as your skills evolve.

The Quest for Continual Learning and Improvement

1. Lifelong Learning:
   - Evolving Craft: Lampworking is an art form that continuously evolves. Staying committed to learning keeps you in tune with new methods, materials, and artistic trends.
   - Workshops and Community: Engaging in workshops, community forums, and collaborations exposes you to diverse perspectives and techniques, enriching your own practice.

2. Refinement and Mastery:
   - Advancing Skills: The journey of skill development is never-ending. Even the most experienced artists find room for improvement and

refinement.

- Sharing Knowledge: As you grow in your art, sharing your knowledge and experiences with others can be a rewarding way to give back to the lampworking community.

The journey from a beginner to an intermediate lampworker and beyond is a blend of mastering techniques, embracing challenges, and continually seeking growth and improvement. It is a journey marked not just by what you create with glass and flame but by the skills, insights, and artistic vision you develop along the way.

Introduction to the Series by the Author

Hello and welcome! I'm Jenelle Aubade, your guide and fellow artist on this exciting journey through the art of glass lampworking. As someone deeply immersed in this craft for many years, I'm thrilled to share with you my new book series, "Modern Lampwork Recipes - Fire and Glass." This series is a labor of love, born from my passion for glass art and my desire to share the knowledge and experience I've gathered over the years.

Purpose of the Series

The primary goal of this series is to inspire and educate. Each volume is crafted to not only provide detailed, recipe-style instructions for creating beautiful lampwork pieces but also to encourage you to explore your creativity within a structured framework. Think of these books as a palette of possibilities - a starting point for you to experiment, innovate, and infuse your personal artistic flair into each creation.

In these pages, you'll find a blend of technique, artistry, and practical advice, all aimed at enhancing your skills and broadening your understanding of the lampworking process. Whether it's exploring the nuances of color, understanding the interplay of materials, or mastering the precision of the flame, this series is designed to take your lampworking to new heights.

Structure of the Series

The series is thoughtfully structured into twelve volumes, each focused on a different color palette. From the fiery reds and oranges of "Jubilee" to the tranquil blues and greens of "Sparkling Tides," every book offers a unique exploration of colors and their application in lampworking. This structured approach allows you to delve deep into specific color themes, understanding their characteristics, and learning how to effectively incorporate them into your glass art.

Target Audience

This series is tailored for intermediate glass artists like you, who already possess a foundational understanding of lampworking. If you're familiar with the basics of this craft and are looking to expand your skills and artistic range, these books are an ideal fit. I've designed each volume to build upon your existing knowledge, challenging you to push your boundaries and explore new aspects of lampworking.

Whether you're looking to refine your techniques, explore new styles, or simply find inspiration for your next project, this series offers a wealth of knowledge and insights. It's a journey of artistic growth, and I'm so excited to embark on it together with you.

Approach and Content

As we delve into the heart of this series, I want to give you a clear picture of what to expect from each book, both in terms of format and content. My aim is to provide a balanced mix of detailed guidance, artistic inspiration, and an invitation for your creativity to flourish.

Recipe-Style Format

Each book in this series adopts a recipe-style format, a concept that I find beautifully suited to the art of lampworking. Just as a cooking recipe guides you through creating a delicious dish, these lampwork "recipes" will guide you through the creation of stunning glass pieces. Every "recipe" includes:

- List of Materials: Detailed information on the types of glass and other materials needed.
  - Step-by-Step Instructions: Clear, concise directions that walk you through the process from start to finish.
  - Visual Aids: Wherever possible, I've included diagrams to help you visualize each step and the expected outcomes.

This format is designed to be both informative and easy to follow, ensuring you can recreate each piece while understanding the technique behind it.

Focus on Color and Design Palettes

Color is the soul of lampworking. Each volume of this series is dedicated to a specific color or design palette, allowing for a deep exploration of its potential in glass art. From the fiery hues in "Spice" to the serene tones in "Danube," every book is an exploration of how color can be manipulated, combined, and showcased in lampwork beads.

But it's not just about color. Alongside, you'll find focus on various design elements – textures, patterns, and forms – that complement the color schemes. This holistic approach ensures that each creation is not just a demonstration of color theory but also a testament to thoughtful design.

Balancing Instruction, Inspiration, and Creativity

A crucial aspect of this series is finding the perfect balance between instruction, inspiration, and creativity. While the step-by-step recipes provide the structure and guidance needed for creating specific pieces, I strongly encourage you to infuse your personality and style into each project.

Consider the instructions as a starting point – a foundation upon which you can build your unique creations. I hope that each book not only teaches you new techniques but also inspires you to experiment and push the boundaries of your art. Your creative interpretation is what will make each piece truly your own.

In crafting this series, my goal is to guide, inspire, and ignite your passion for lampworking. Each book is a stepping stone in your artistic journey, offering the knowledge and inspiration you need to create beautiful, expressive glass art. I can't wait to see the incredible pieces you'll create and the unique ways you'll make these recipes your own.

Invitation

As we reach the end of this introduction, I extend a heartfelt invitation to you, my fellow lampworking enthusiasts. This series is more than just a collection of instructions and techniques; it's a doorway into a world of artistic freedom and community engagement.

I wholeheartedly encourage you to view these books not just as guides, but as springboards for experimentation. The techniques and designs I present are adaptable, meant to be tweaked and reinvented by your own creative hands. Don't hesitate to stray from the path, to mix, match, and morph these ideas into something that resonates with your personal artistic vision. Remember, every great artist once dared to deviate from the norm, and in that daring, they discovered their unique voice.

The Communal and Evolving Nature of Lampworking

Lampworking, at its core, is a communal art form, enriched and sustained by the contributions of its practitioners. I urge you to embrace this collaborative spirit. Share your work, your successes, and even your challenges. Engage with the lampworking community – both locally and online – to exchange ideas, techniques, and stories. This shared journey of discovery and improvement is what keeps the art of lampworking vibrant and ever-evolving.

Feedback, Sharing of Results, and Community Engagement

Your feedback and experiences are invaluable. I invite you to share your creations and insights derived from this series. Whether it's through social media, online forums, or community gatherings, let's create a dialogue that celebrates our successes and learns from our experiences. Your participation is what will truly bring this series to life.

As we embark on this exciting journey together, I am filled with anticipation to see how you will take these recipes and transform them into expressions of your own artistic journey. Your creativity is the final, crucial ingredient in each piece you create. Lampworking is not just about mastering the flame and the glass; it's about igniting the fire of creativity within yourself.

I am honored to be a part of your lampworking journey and look forward to seeing your incredible creations. Remember, in the world of glass and flame, each day is an opportunity to create something beautiful, something uniquely yours.

Let's keep the flames of creativity burning bright and share the warmth and beauty of our art with the world.

Warmly,

Jenelle Aubade

Acknowledgement

At the heart of every great endeavor lies the support and inspiration we draw from those around us. As I bring this series, "Modern Lampwork Recipes - Fire and Glass," into your hands, it is with a profound sense of gratitude that I acknowledge the contributions of those who have been instrumental in this journey.

First and foremost, I extend my deepest thanks to Daniel Caracas, my partner in both life and art. Daniel's creative genius is the bedrock upon which many of the designs in this series stand. His meticulous approach to lampworking and his innate ability to conjure intricate designs from the flame have been nothing short of inspiring. We share more than a studio and resources; we share a passion for glass that intertwines our lives and work in a dance of creativity and discovery.

Many of the designs you will encounter throughout these pages are the fruits of Daniel's artistic vision. His unique and impeccable style, coupled with our collaborative spirit, has allowed these creations to flourish. It is both an honor and a privilege to present some of his most celebrated designs here, with his generous permission.

I also wish to thank the lampworking community—artists, hobbyists, and enthusiasts alike—for their unwavering support and endless inspiration. This series is a tribute to our collective journey in glass, a testament to the boundless creativity and solidarity that thrives within our ranks.

To our friends and family, who have witnessed the sparks of our torches late into the night and have encouraged our artistic pursuits—your belief in our work fuels our ambition and dedication.

Lastly, to you, the reader and fellow artist, for embarking on this adventure with us. Your enthusiasm for learning and pushing the boundaries of lampwork art is the ultimate motivation for sharing our knowledge and experience.

May this series not only serve as a guide but also as a source of inspiration for your own creative path in the mesmerizing world of lampworking.

With heartfelt appreciation,

Jenelle Aubade

About Jubilee

A Celebration of Warm Hues and Lustrous Details

Welcome to "Jubilee," the first volume in our 'Modern Lampwork Recipes - Fire and Glass' series. In this opening chapter, we embark on a journey through a palette rich in warmth and elegance, where the dance of light and color comes alive in each bead we create.

Introducing Jubilee's Unique Designs

In "Jubilee," we will explore three distinct designs, each unified by a mesmerizing color palette that evokes the richness of a warm plum sunset. Imagine the luxurious interplay of fine silver over creamy ivory, the subtle glint of fine silver details, and the deep, enchanting shimmer of goldstone aventurine, all encased in the pristine clarity of Italian crystal glass. These elements combine to create beads that are not just components but tiny, wearable pieces of art.

Versatility in Design and Application

Crafted on 5mm bead mandrels, these designs are perfect for larger scale projects. Whether it's adorning show dog leads with a touch of elegance, adding a unique flair to macrame creations, serving as statement pieces in dreadlocks, or threading through leather or ribbons, these beads are designed to stand out. Their size and presence make them ideal for bold expressions of style.

However, the beauty of "Jubilee" lies in its adaptability. While we focus on larger beads, these designs can effortlessly transition to smaller mandrels, catering to a bead hole size of 2mm. This flexibility ensures that the techniques and styles you learn here can be applied to a variety of bead shapes and sizes, making them suitable for a wide range of jewelry designs.

A Canvas for Creativity

As we delve into each recipe, I encourage you to view these designs not just as instructions but as starting points for your own creative exploration.

About Jubilee

The "Jubilee" collection is more than a set of designs; it's an invitation to experiment with shapes, sizes, and applications. Let these recipes inspire you to adapt and infuse your personality into each piece you create.

Prepare to immerse yourself in the world of "Jubilee," where each bead tells a story of warmth, opulence, and creativity. This is just the beginning of our journey together, and I can't wait to see how you bring these designs to life in your own unique way. Let's turn the torch on and start this beautiful adventure in lampworking!

Jubilee Round Duo

Jubilee Round Duo

Discover the Jubilee Round Duo, where rustic charm meets celestial wonder in a harmonious rondelle shape. These beads, crafted on a generous 5mm mandrel, boast a substantial presence, ranging from 10-12mm in height and 14-15mm in width, perfect for statement pieces that command attention.

Each bead presents a tale of two halves: one, a rustic ivory canvas, speckled with twinkling fine silver that mimics a starlit night sky. This metallic luster brings a lively sparkle, adding visual interest and an ancient allure to the design. The other half is a captivating dance of warm plum hues, a frit blend that swirls and suspends within the crystal-clear encasement, invoking the majesty of a sunset trapped in glass.

This dichotomy is unified by a layer of pristine Italian crystal glass, enveloping the colors and textures in a depth that invites the eye to explore and linger. The clear encasement is not merely a protective layer; it is a window into the bead's soul, magnifying the intricate details and elevating the overall aesthetic.

Originally designed for the ornate leashes of show dogs and the unique adornment of dreadlocks, the Jubilee Round Duo transcends its initial purpose. These beads flourish as the crowning jewel in bohemian long knotted necklaces, adding a touch of antiquity and opulence. Their versatile nature allows them to be scaled down, using smaller mandrels for a variety of jewelry designs, ensuring that the Jubilee Round Duo can be a signature piece for many creations.

The Jubilee Round is not just a bead; it's a versatile component that carries a spirit of celebration and ageless beauty, ready to be woven into your narrative of craftsmanship and design.

Getting Started with Jubilee Round Duo

As we embark on the creation of the Jubilee Round Duo beads, it's time to gather the select materials that will bring these pieces to life. Each component has been carefully chosen for its quality and contribution to the aesthetic and structural integrity of the beads.

Ingredients List

1. Ivory Glass - Light, Effetre: Begin with a base of Effetre's light ivory glass, which offers a versatile and classic backdrop for your design.

2. Heavy Fine Silver Foil: This will be our accent feature, providing a shimmering contrast against the ivory with its reflective properties. *GlassDiversions.com

3. Pastel White Glass: This will make the frit blend color pop!
3. Clear Glass - Effetre Super Clear from Italy: Use this for encasing your beads, giving them a glossy finish and magnifying the intricate details within.

4. Grapes Galore Frit Blend - by Glass Diversions: Add depth and a burst of color with this frit blend, rich in warm plum tones for a vibrant effect. *GlassDiversions.com

5. Goldstone Aventurine Chunk: Pulled into a fine stringer, this material will introduce a glittering, coppery streak for a hint of sparkle.

6. .999 Fine Silver Wire - by Rio Grand: Incorporate fine silver wire to create small, reflective surface details to the bead, adding visual depth and enhancing its luxurious feel.

With these high-quality materials ready, we're set to begin the rewarding process of crafting the Jubilee Round Duo beads. Each step will take us closer to completing a bead that is as functional as it is beautiful, perfect for a variety of uses from jewelry to decorative accents.

Step-by-Step RECIPE

As we craft the Jubilee Round Duo beads, we'll embrace a blend of the tried-and-true with a hint of innovation. Keep an eye out for how each material, from the reactive silver to the lustrous goldstone, brings its own character to the bead under the careful orchestration of the flame.

1. Prepare Your Mandrel:
   - Start with a large hole bead mandrel prepped with bead release. Air or flame-dry the coating to ensure it's fully set.

2. Create the Ivory Footprint:
   - Melt the Light Ivory glass and wind a foundational footprint onto the mandrel, forming the first half of your bead's base.

3. Apply Silver Foil:
   - Heat the ivory footprint slightly and press it onto a piece of .999 heavy silver foil. Ensure the silver is smoothly attached.

4. Add a White Glass Footprint:
   - Before moving on, add a small footprint of white glass on the mandrel beside the ivory. This will act as a canvas to make the colors of the frit pop in the next step.

5. Prepare the Frit-Infused Glass:
   - In a neutral flame, heat the tip of a clear glass rod until it's ready to melt but not flowing. Dip it into the Grapes Galore frit blend to coat it generously and melt in lightly until smooth.

6. Apply the Frit Glass Footprint:
   - Heat and carefully wrap the frit-coated clear glass around the white footprint you just made, forming the second half of your bead.

7. Incorporate the Goldstone Stringer:
   - Warm the tip of a goldstone stringer and apply a delicate band around the bead's midpoint, dividing the ivory and frit glass sections. Monitor the heat to preserve the goldstone's bright sparkle.

8. Encase with Clear Glass:
   - With a steady hand, cover the entire bead in a thin layer of Effetre Super

Clear glass. Use the heat and gravity to shape it into a rondelle, ensuring even coverage and smoothness.

9. Final Shaping:
   - Continue to perfect the rondelle shape, paying close attention to achieving a harmonious balance, good dimples, and a flawless surface.

10. Embellish with Fine Silver Wire:
    - As a final touch, wrap .999 fine silver wire around the center of the bead. The wire will melt into tiny droplets, adding a layer of depth and texture to your design.

11. Anneal the Bead:
    - Place the finished bead into the kiln, set to the appropriate annealing temperature, to stabilize and solidify your work.

Diagram - shown horizontally as the beads would be placed on your mandrel during creation. My instructions cover creating one bead, but feel free to make two or more on the same mandrel if your skills are raring to go.

- A & B: ivory footprint with the silver foil wrapped around it.
- C: Highlights the addition of the white glass footprint before the frit application.
- D: Illustrates the bead with the frit-coated clear glass wrapped around the white footprint.
- E: Displays the placement of the goldstone stringer.
- F: Displays the placement of the fine silver wire.

With these steps in mind, allow the process to unfold naturally, and enjoy the alchemy of glass and silver coming together in your hands.

Implementation and Marketing Ideas

The Jubilee Round Duo beads, with their large holes and bold design, are not just standalone beauties; they are versatile players in the wider world of art and fashion. Envision them as the focal point in a statement necklace, the bold finish on a luxurious show dog lead, or even as unique embellishments in a boho-chic macrame wall hanging. Their size and the visual impact make them ideal for designs where you want the bead to take center stage.

Marketing to Potential Customers

In presenting these beads to potential buyers or jewelry designers, highlight their versatility and the story behind their creation. High-quality images that show off the depth and sparkle of the beads can captivate your audience. Consider creating sample pieces that showcase how these beads can be used, providing immediate inspiration. At craft shows or in your online store, display them prominently as premium offerings, emphasizing their handcrafted nature and the uniqueness of each bead.

Customer Use Cases

Real-life applications from my regular customers include these beads being used as elegant counterweights on decorative fan pulls, as luxe zipper pulls on designer handbags, and as distinctive accents on bridal accessories. They have been incorporated into custom jewelry pieces for special occasions, speaking to their allure and the distinct touch they add to any creation.

Inspirational Thoughts

As we wrap up this recipe, remember that the true beauty of lampworking lies in the personal touch you bring to every bead. I encourage you to let your creativity flow freely, taking the foundation laid here and building upon it with your own style and flair.

I'd love to see the unique ways you bring the Jubilee Round beads to life. Share your creations and stories with the community, and let's inspire each other with our shared passion for glass art. Whether on social media, online forums, or at community events, your work adds to the collective tapestry of our craft.

Keep the flame burning, and let every bead tell its story.

Jubilee Barrel

Jubilee Silver and Ivory

W elcome to the next step in our creative series with the Jubilee Barrel Focal Bead. Building on the familiar materials from the Round Duo, this bead elevates your craft with its distinct, hand-shaped form and added visual dynamics. It's a piece that not only stands out due to its size but also due to the intricate details that you'll be able to bring to life.

The Jubilee Barrel Focal Bead is a substantial piece, allowing for more surface area to showcase the contrasting textures and colors. It's a bead that invites a second glance, with two spiraled rows of goldstone creating wave-like patterns on its surface, reminiscent of gilded crests on a calm sea. This touch of goldstone, set against the depth of warm plum and textured ivory, provides a multifaceted appearance that catches the light—and the eye.

This design offers you the keys to create a bead that will be the heart of any jewelry piece, a focal point that draws attention and complements both casual wear and more formal ensembles. It's designed to be a showstopper, encouraging jewelry designers to feature it in pieces that their customers will be proud to wear and display.

By following this recipe, you'll unlock the potential to craft beads that resonate with your clients, beads that add a touch of luxury to their collections. The Jubilee Barrel Focal Bead is more than just a component; it's a gateway to new possibilities in your lampworking artistry and a design that will delight and inspire your clientele.

INGREDIENTS - same as the Jubilee rounds, but be sure to pull a clear stringer before getting started, and make sure you have enough goldstone stringer pulled to wrap around the bead twice =)

Step-by-Step Recipe

In crafting the Jubilee Barrel Focal Bead, we create a piece that stands as a testament to the elegance and stature of a true focal point. Measuring approximately 12-13mm in width by 30-34mm in length, this bead is especially suited as a centerpiece for show dog leads, offering a touch of grandeur and intricate detail that is sure to stand out. Create the design on a smaller 2mm bead mandrel and/or other bead shapes for lots of jewelry designing options.

1. Mandrel Preparation:
   - Begin with a large hole mandrel coated with bead release. Ensure the release is completely dry before you start.

2. Initial White Footprint:
   - Apply a thin strip of white glass around the mandrel to mark the length of your finished bead. This serves as the foundation for the design.

3. Ivory Center:
   - Wrap a band of ivory glass around the middle section of the white base. Heat it until it's warm but not fully melted in and roll the band in heavy fine silver foil.

4. Frit-Infused Ends:
   - Add the Grapes Galore frit-dipped clear glass to both ends of the bead, adjacent to the ivory section, to frame the centerpiece.

5. Initial Shaping:
   - Gently melt the entire design in, ensuring a smooth integration of colors and textures. Use a marver to flatten and refine the surface.

6. Clear Glass Encasement:
   - Encase the entire bead in clear glass. Taper the ends by using less glass if desired, creating a more defined barrel shape.

7. Refining the Barrel Shape:
   - Add clear glass and shape until you achieve a pleasing barrel form, ensuring even distribution and proper dimpling at the ends.

8. Goldstone Stringer Application:
   - Wrap goldstone stringer around the ends where the frit-dipped glass meets the ivory. This not only conceals the seam but also adds a touch of luxury. Immediately place a thin line of clear glass on top of the goldstone to save the sparkle. Melt the design in and reshape as needed.

9. Wave Creation:
   - To form the waves, heat a small section of the goldstone stringer section and press the cold tip of a clear glass stringer against it. Once attached, twist to create a wave shape, pause to let it cool slightly, then snap off the stringer from the bead. I rap the stringer against the end of my torch for this part. Repeat this process around both of the goldstone sections.

10. Refinement and Reshaping:
    - After the waves are formed, carefully melt them back into the bead, reshaping as necessary to maintain the barrel silhouette.

11. Fine Silver Droplets:
    - Wrap a generous amount of fine silver wire around the central ivory section. Heat until the wire forms small droplets on the surface, enhancing the bead's texture.

12. Kiln Annealing:
    - Place the completed bead into the kiln to anneal, ensuring its durability and longevity.

Remember to take your time with each step, allowing the materials to blend seamlessly under the flame. The process is just as rewarding as beholding the final, stunning Jubilee Barrel Focal Bead, ready to be the centerpiece of a beautiful creation.

See the BONUS section for examples of this size bead in design.

Jubilee Organics

S tep into the world of the Jubilee Organics, a bead design that embraces the natural allure and tactile beauty of organic shapes. This design is a cornerstone of versatility, primarily serving as an exquisite complement to show dog lead designs, lariat necklaces, and as eye-catching closures for knotted bead strands. When adorned in dreadlocks, these beads add a unique, artistic touch that is both functional and stylish.

Crafted with the same premium materials as the other designs in the Jubilee series, the Jubilee Organics bring something extra to the table. Their final form is distinguished by a hand-faceted style that not only plays with light like faceted gemstones but also offers a delightful textural experience to the touch. These beads are not merely seen; they are felt, engaging the senses with every facet and glint.

When scaled down and threaded onto smaller mandrels, the Jubilee Organics open up a myriad of possibilities for jewelry designers. They transform into versatile components that can dance along with a delicate bracelet or hang elegantly from a pair of earrings, offering endless creative potential.

The Jubilee Organics are a testament to the craftsmanship and innovation that lampworking can achieve. They are a celebration of the unique beauty that comes from hand-shaped, thoughtfully faceted glass, destined to capture both the light and the admirers' gaze.

INGREDIENTS - same as the Jubilee rounds, but omit the goldstone.
Extra Tool! I use a shaping tool from ABR Imagery to create the surface texture for this design. Use a stainless steel or brass knife/shaping tool to recreate it.
The Secret to Shaping Glass Organics - Crafting the Signature Facets

Creating the Jubilee Organics is an experience that blends the methodical aspects of lampworking with the artistry of hand-finishing. Once you have crafted the round bead to your satisfaction, the transformation into a uniquely faceted organic gem begins. This final touch is where your personal style truly shines through, leaving an artisanal mark on each bead.

Creating the Faceted Effect

1. Spot Heating:
   - Begin by gently heating the surface of the bead in specific areas. The goal is to soften the glass just enough to manipulate, without affecting the overall shape or design underneath.

2. Indention Technique:
   - With a stainless steel or brass shaping tool, press into the surface of the warm glass to create indentations. The depth and angle at which you press will contribute to the final appearance of the facets.

3. Artistry in Imperfection:
   - Embrace randomness in your indentations to maintain the organic feel. The beauty of the Jubilee Organics lies in their one-of-a-kind nature, with each bead bearing the unique touch of its creator.

4. Pressure and Posture:
   - The pressure you apply and the curve of your hand posture during this process will ensure no two beads are exactly alike. Your individual technique will naturally imbue the beads with your signature style.

5. Valuing Uniqueness:
   - This hand-faceted approach not only adds to the tactile and visual charm of the beads but also increases their value as collectors' items. Each bead is a stand-alone piece, reflecting the time-honored tradition of handcrafted artistry.

The Collection

Over 15 years ago, I conceived and crafted this design, which has since blossomed into a beloved collection. My long bohemian knotted bead strand necklaces, featuring my signature glass Organics, are a testament to the enduring appeal of this style. The beads add a modern and unique touch to each piece, ensuring they stand out in any jewelry collection.

The process of making these beads is as enjoyable as it is creative, offering a modern twist on traditional lampwork beads. As you finish each Jubilee Organic bead, take pleasure in the knowledge that you are creating something truly contemporary, a piece that will be treasured for its artistry and innovation. Enjoy the process, and let your style be reflected in every facet you form.

Examples : Organics

Jubilee Organics

Resources

Resource Section for "Modern Lampwork Recipes - Fire and Glass"

In this series, we've explored the intricate and beautiful world of lampworking. To help you continue your journey, I've compiled a list of resources that I personally use and recommend. These tools and suppliers have been integral in my own lampworking process, and I hope they will assist you in your creative endeavors as well.

Tools I Use

1. Kilns:
   - Paragon Bluebird and SC-2: Renowned for their reliability and precision, these kilns are essential for quality bead annealing.

2. Mandrels & Shaping Tools:
   - I source my mandrels and shaping tools from reputable suppliers like Mountain Glass , ABR Imagery , and Frantz Glass . These tools are fundamental for creating beads with precision and beauty.

3. Torch:
   - Carlisle Mini CC : This torch is a staple in my studio, offering the perfect

balance of control and power for detailed work.

Glass & Frit Suppliers

1. Mountain Glass: A reliable source for high-quality glass and supplies.
2. Frantz Art Glass : Offers a wide selection of colors and types of glass.
3. Val Cox Frit: Specializes in beautiful, unique frit blends.
4. Glass Diversions: A great source for frit and other lampworking materials. This is also where I get my Silver Foil.
5. Rio Grande - .999 fine silver wire, round, dead soft, .30 gauge

Classes

Interested in learning more and honing your skills in a hands-on environment? Daniel and I offer private lampworking classes in our home studio in Todos Santos, Baja Sur, Mexico. Our classes run from November through April each year, and we welcome students of all levels. For more information and to sign up, visit BajaTiki - Lampwork Classes.

About Us and Our Glass Studio

Since 2006, my husband Daniel Caracas and I have been immersed in the art of making glass lampwork beads. Originally from the USA, we now find ourselves in the sunny, serene town of Todos Santos on the Baja penninsula in Mexico. Our tiny pueblo town not only inspires our work but also serves as the backdrop for our home studio.

In our studio, Daniel specializes in creating large scenic and ornate beads, each a miniature masterpiece. My focus lies in small organically shaped beads, where I explore the nuances of color and form. Together, we strive to push the boundaries of lampworking, constantly exploring new techniques and styles.

Our passion extends beyond our own creations. We love sharing our knowledge and skills with others, which is why we offer private lampworking classes. These classes are an opportunity for us to connect with fellow

Resources

enthusiasts, share our love for glass art, and help others develop their skills.

Whether you're just starting your journey in lampworking or looking to refine your techniques, we hope the resources and classes we offer will help you on your path. Remember, the world of lampworking is as vast as it is beautiful, and there's always something new to discover.

Happy lampworking, and may your creativity continue to shine bright!

Warm regards,

Jenelle Aubade and Daniel Caracas
Paradise Lampwork @ BAJTIKI.com

BONUS : Additional Design Examples

A dditional Design Examples: A Bonus Section

Welcome to the "Additional Design Examples" page, a special bonus section in each volume of our "Modern Lampwork Recipes - Fire and Glass" series. This section is a visual feast, an exclusive peek into the extensive catalog of my bead designs that resonate with the themes and techniques of the current tutorial.

A Showcase of Creativity and Versatility

In this section, you'll find a curated collection of photographs showcasing a variety of bead designs. These pieces have been carefully selected to complement and expand upon the techniques and materials discussed in the main tutorials. Each design is a testament to the versatility of lampworking and serves as a source of inspiration and ideas for your own creations.

Discover New Possibilities

As you browse through these examples, notice how different elements and techniques come together to create unique and captivating beads. You may recognize some of the materials and methods from the tutorials, applied in new and innovative ways. This section is designed to spark your imagination, encouraging you to explore the endless possibilities within the art of lampworking.

Connect Techniques with Artistry

The Additional Design Examples page bridges the gap between technique and artistry. By seeing how the same ingredients can be utilized to produce diverse aesthetic results, you'll gain a deeper understanding of the creative potential that lies within each lampwork recipe.

A Continuous Source of Inspiration

Consider this section as a continuous source of inspiration, a place to return to whenever you need a creative boost or a fresh perspective. Whether it's a unique color combination, an intriguing shape, or an unexpected texture, these designs are here to ignite your creativity and enrich your lampworking journey.

BONUS : *Additional Design Examples*

Embrace the ideas and inspiration within these pages, and let them guide you as you bring your own vision to life in the flame. Happy creating, and I hope these designs add an extra layer of joy and discovery to your lampworking experience!

BONUS : Additional Design Examples

Afterward

A Journey Through Glass and Fire

As we close this chapter of our vibrant journey through the art of lampworking, I want to extend my heartfelt gratitude for joining me in this creative exploration. "Modern Lampwork Recipes - Fire and Glass" has been a journey of color, light, and imagination, and your participation has made it all the more enriching.

Staying Connected

Should you have any questions, thoughts, or stories you'd like to share about your experience with these recipes, I am just a click away. Feel free to reach out via my website: www.Jenelle.Rocks/Glass. Your feedback, inquiries, and insights are not only welcome but also a valuable part of our continuing lampworking adventure.

Explore More Designs

For those who wish to delve deeper into the world of glass art, I invite you to explore my other bead designs and collections. You can find a treasure trove of inspiration and beauty at:

- [BajaTiki.com](#)
- **Facbook Groups**:
    - [Paradise Beads](#)
    - [Lampwork Jewelry and Bead Auctions](#)
    - [Heart Of Glass Jewelry](#)
    - [Amazing Glass](#)

- **Facbook Pages**:
    - [Art Glass Beads](#)
    - [Jenelle Aubade](#)

- **Instagram**:
    - [@JenelleAubade](#)
    - [@paradiselampwork](#)
    - [@heartofglassjewelry](#)

Discover My Literary World

For those who are avid readers and wish to explore more of my work beyond glass art, I invite you to visit my author page on Amazon: [Jenelle Aubade - Amazon Author](#) - Here, you'll find a collection of my books and novels, each a journey into different realms of creativity and storytelling.

Connect on Other Platforms

And for a more comprehensive view of my world, check out:
- [Linktree](#)
- [Bio.site](#)

Thank you for allowing me to be a part of your lampworking journey. The flames of creativity burn brightest when shared, and I am delighted to have shared this experience with you. Keep the torch lit, keep experimenting, and most importantly, keep creating. Until our paths cross again in the wondrous world of glass art, happy lampworking!

Warm regards,

Jenelle Aubade
www.Jenelle.Rocks

www.ingramcontent.com/pod-product-compliance
Ingram Content Group UK Ltd.
Pitfield, Milton Keynes, MK11 3LW, UK
UKHW051627151025
8403UKWH00022B/135